FROM THE PROJECTS TO THE
PROMISED LAND

developing a recipe & road map for your life

TONYA LATNEY

© 2013 Tonya Latney. All rights reserved.

No part of this book may be reproduced, stored in a retrieval system, or transmitted by any means without the written permission of the author.

Printed in the United States of America.

This book is printed on acid-free paper.

Any people depicted in stock imagery provided by Thinkstock are models, and such images are being used for illustrative purposes only.

Certain stock imagery © Thinkstock.

Scripture taken from the New King James Version. Copyright 1979, 1980, 1982 by Thomas Nelson, inc. Used by permission. All rights reserved.

Because of the dynamic nature of the Internet, any web addresses or links contained in this book may have changed since publication and may no longer be valid.

I was encouraged by a friend to write this book. She felt that my life could be an encouragement to other women in various areas of their lives. I hope that after reading this book, women can find their way to become the person they want to become, or that they can get back on track as the person they started to become earlier in their life.

The goal of this book is to get you to stop and think about your life and the path you are traveling. Will the path you are traveling lead you to your promised land?

Thank you, Mrs. Elaine Fulton, for seeing what I did not see.

TABLE OF CONTENTS

Introduction ix

Chapter 1   Stop 1

Chapter 2   The Recipe and Road Map 10

Chapter 3   The Dream 29

Chapter 4   Your Attitude 35

Chapter 5   Trapped 45

Chapter 6   Keep It Moving 57

Chapter 7   Season, Reason, Lifetime 69

Chapter 8   Success 80

Chapter 9   Staying Beautiful 86

Chapter 10   The Promised Land 92

Endnotes 101

INTRODUCTION

This book is titled *From the Projects to the Promised Land*. What is a promise? The Wikipedia definition of a promise is as follows: "A promise is a commitment by someone to do or not do something." What are projects? The urban dictionary defines "projects" as "a place where black people are born, raised, and eventually killed." Sad to say, that is what most people think about projects. However, the Wikipedia definition is as follows: "Public housing is a form of housing tenure in which the property is owned by a government authority, which may be central or local. Although the common goal of public housing is to provide affordable housing, the details, terminology, definitions of poverty and other criteria for allocation vary within different contexts."

Everyone's journey may start in a different place; mine started in the projects. And not everyone has the same promised land; mine is to help women all over the world. Your promised land is what you want it to be. The promised land is your commitment to yourself as to where you are going in life; it is where you set your road map to take you. There are many good people who go through life with no destination in mind. Do you have a destination? Remember, life is a journey and should start with a beginning and have a destination.

Have you taken the time to make a promise of where you want to go in life, how to get to your promised land? The first step you must take is to decide how to start your journey to your promised land. This process consists of you asking yourself questions such as, Who am I? Am I happy with who I am, and if not, who do I want to become? Where do I want to go in life? What does my promised land look like? and What will it take for me to reach my promised land?

The second thing you are going to do is make a big decision—and I say "big" because whenever you decide to make a change in your life's direction, it is big; it will take motivation, dedication, and focus. "Motivation," "dedication," and "focus" are the three words you will need to get you to your promised land.

My belief is that everyone has a purpose in life; however, many people live their entire life not knowing what that purpose is. Do you think you have a purpose in life? I came to know that my purpose is to help women achieve their purpose, plans, and passion in their lives. When I started asking myself the questions above, it started the journey that I was intended to walk in.

My journey started when I was fifteen, pregnant, and living in the projects. Who would have thought that my experiences from then to today would help other women? Not I. Who would have thought God could call me to teach and guide other females? Not I. I realized that my mission in life became my ministry. The pain became my plan. You see, it took me a minute to realize that many of the challenging events that I encountered on my journey were not a punishment, but part of God's plan. God's plan was to take me from the projects to the promised land to use me for the kingdom to help other women. God has allowed me to go through a journey in this game called life. He has used me and my life as an example of his goodness and faithfulness; he has allowed my test to become a testimony that I can use to reach back and pull another woman up.

I hope that after reading this book you will have an understanding that no matter what life throws your way, you can achieve your goals.

This book is intended to be an easy, quick read to help you to start thinking about the changes you need to make to reach the goal of your promised land.

Each chapter ends with reflection questions that you should take the time to answer. One of the things I found to be very helpful in achieving my dreams and goals was journaling, so these reflection pages are there for you to search your soul and write down what's going on inside of you. I believe that writing helps to bring change, so the reflection pages are there for that reason—for you to write your personal thoughts relating to what you have read. Journaling is a great tool for growth and reflection. It allows you to go back and read and see growth in your journey.

Let's begin the journey to the new you!

CHAPTER 1
Stop

While growing up, I was a regular kid, but one wrong decision changed me from a kid to an adult seemingly overnight. "I am not scared" were the words that changed my life. Although I love my child, there was a time at which I wished I would have said, "I am scared and I am not ready."

The day came when I had to stop, look, and think. This took place at age fifteen, when I was carrying around a product that I prayed that I would use. However, I did not use it, Yes, a feminine product! I prayed every day, saying, "Please come, please come," and then imagining I had cramps; but there were no cramps, and there was no reason to use the product I was carrying around. Instead what I was carrying was a person whom I had planned not to carry until many years later. The next words I heard were "She is about five months pregnant, maybe six." My mother flipped, and I was in shock. All I could think was, *What happened? I thought I was being careful!* This situation caused me to stop, look, and think. Now you take a moment and think about what caused you—or should have caused you—to stop, look, and think.

Having a baby at age fifteen was a very embarrassing thing. It was not cute being pregnant at this age; however, every day I tried to think positively about me and my situation. It was a very hard situation. Over the years I have heard many people say that having a baby does not change your life, but I am here to tell you that having a baby as a teenager is definitely a life-changing event in every area of your life. It affects you mentally, physically, socially, financially, and emotionally. On many days I looked at my son and said, "What am I going to do with a child?" But then one day I looked at my son and looked at myself and made a decision. That decision was to be the best person I could be.

When I made this decision, I again had to take time to stop, look, and think about my environment and direction. Did you ever take the time to stop and look at your surroundings, your environment, and your life? In order to have an understanding about who you are, what you are, and where you want to go in life, you must stop, look, and think. Anyone who plans to make positive changes in her life should follow the principle of stop, look, and think. This principle may help you avoid making decisions in your life that could come back to haunt or hurt you later.

As children we are taught the stop, look, and think principle about what we are doing; however, many times when we think about this principle, it is related to teaching us how to cross a street by stopping at the corner and looking both ways. Why are we taught this principle at such a young age? We are taught this principle to prevent us from getting hit by a moving vehicle, such as a car, truck, bus, or bike—anything that crosses our path while we try to walk across the street. This principle is a way in which we are protected from getting hurt, injured, or even killed. In your life, how many times have you felt as though you have been hit by a moving object? Well, if you have not already had this feeling, be careful, because if are you not taking the time to stop, look, and think, you will have this feeling sooner or later. The principle of stop, look, and think will play a major role throughout your life.

I can remember making a decision without stopping and thinking when I was nine years old. I received one of the worst butt whuppings ever! We were living on the ninth floor of a high-rise building in the projects. Each day, my mother would call me from the balcony when it was time for me to come in from outside. Well, this particular day I decided to ignore her calling me, because I was having fun with my friends and I was not ready to go in the house. Well, she finally came outside to look for me. When she found me, she asked, "Did you hear me calling you?" I quickly said yes, and I think I said something along the lines of "I didn't feel like coming in the house." To this day, when I look at the scar that is on my thigh, I remember that incident. I will never forget that day; I wish that I had stopped talking and thought before I responded. When my mother and I talk about that scar today, it's funny, but it was not funny then. That is my story. I bet you have your own stories—some funny and some not so funny.

There will come a time in your life when you must stop, look, and think. That time comes at different moments for different people, and surprisingly enough it never happens at all for some, which may be a major part of many problems in one's life.

Stopping allows you time to think about who you are, who you want to be in life, and what you are supposed to do with your life. What is your purpose for living? Do you believe that you were created to wake up daily, go to work, come home, and just pay bills? Well, for some that answer may be yes, but for those who say no, there is more to life for you, and by reading this book you are getting on the right track to change things in your life. Have you ever thought about when your life has ended and the obituary states, "Sunrise (your birth date) to sunset (the day you took your last breath)"? What will the dash in between the two mean for you? If your answer is "I do not know," I am not surprised, because many people don't think that far ahead or that deeply, but now that your eyes are open, it is time to make that dash mean something. When you take time to stop, look, and think about your life, you can address many of the questions about your life. If you do not stop, you will just move from day to day with no purpose or plan.

For me, having a baby at age fifteen became a serious thing for me. I thought, *How can I take care of someone when I cannot take care of myself?* I had just started high school; I was in the ninth grade. I did not have a job; my mother was my financial support. I was not even old enough to have a job. How could I be a leader and tell someone where to go when I didn't know where I was going. This was when I really stopped, looked, and thought about my future and future of the child I was going to be responsible for.

During this stopping process, there are many things in your life that need to be addressed, reviewed, and evaluated. Stop what you are doing and take a moment to look in the mirror and ask yourself, "What do I see, and who am I?"

Once you have done this, I am sure you will start thinking about your life in a different manner. Looking at your life requires using a serious eye and honesty, which can be hard for some people to do.

Some of the questions you need to ask yourself are

- Am I happy?
- How is my financial situation?

- How is my educational situation?
- How is my family situation?
- How am I mentally, physically, and spiritually?
- Where do I want to be in life, mentally and physically?
- Where am I living? Is this the state, city, or neighborhood that I want to reside in?

Once you start asking yourself these questions and you find that you are not happy with some of your answers, the next step is to start making changes to those areas that need improvement or change. But the question one may have is, how do I start the process of change? Glad you asked. This is done by creating a recipe and road map for your life.

Take a moment and start by reflecting on what you have done in the past, what you are doing in the present, and what you want from your future. I know this may be hard to do, because most people say, "I don't have time to do this," but if you want a better future and you are ready for change, you must remove from your vocabulary the phrases "I can't" and "I don't have time …" Yes, you can, and you can make time.

As Albert Einstein once said, "The world as we have created it is a process of our thinking. It cannot be changed without changing our thinking." If you are ready to start your new journey and make some changes, remember to take the time to stop, look, and think.

Remember, you are the only person who holds the key to unlock your future.

CHAPTER 1 REFLECTION

Have you ever taken time to stop and think about the direction you are traveling in life?

Are you happy with your life?

Are there any changes you would like to make in your life in any of these areas?

- Finance
- Education
- Family
- Physical health
- Spiritual health
- Mental health
- Place of residence

From the projects to the promised land

"People don't like to think, if one thinks, one must reach conclusions. Conclusions are not always pleasant."

-Helen Keller

PERSONAL REFLECTIONS

CHAPTER 2
The Recipe and Road Map

From the projects to the promised land

You have made a big decision. That decision is to move your life in a direction of wanting better and doing better. In order to do this, you need to write down some things to get you started on the right path. What you will need to write is called a recipe and a road map. Having a recipe and a road map is vital in life; having these two things in place can help you to reach goals so that you may have a more fulfilled and productive life and get to your promised land. How do you begin this process of making a recipe and a road map for your life? Glad you asked.

> Recipe = the ingredients needed to achieve the goal
>
> Road map = the path needed to achieve the goal

Let us begin by defining what a recipe is. A recipe is a list of ingredients that are added together to form a product. The product that we will be focusing on is you.

Writing down your recipe makes it easier for you to follow. When you are baking a cake, for example, you look at the ingredients. Why? Because although you may have baked a cake before, the ingredients might have changed; products are always being improved. If you read a box of cake mix, there are directions on what to do to get to the end product, to make the perfect cake. If your goal is to have a good outcome with the cake, it is suggested that you take the time and follow the directions.

I will use the example of baking a cake in reference to preparing a recipe for your life. I am sure that you have baked a cake in the past. Do you remember that Easy Bake oven many little girls had? Some of us used our mother's pancake mix when we ran out of the cake mix that came with the oven. The only difference in making our cake today is that we will use all the right ingredients.

Once you have all the ingredients, then you can proceed to add them together according to the directions so that your cake batter will be correct. We know that the two things that make a cake come out perfect are the correct ingredients and the temperature of the oven. Life can be similar to baking a cake; you must know the ingredients required to become the person you want to become. Also, the temperature in your environment (which is like the oven) is important. I will discuss this later, but for the moment we will focus on the ingredients. Let's first look at the product you want to become and which ingredients are needed to arrive at this product.

The product is the type of cake you would like to become. I decided I wanted to become a pound cake. I don't know why I chose a pound cake; I guess because it's my favorite cake! It's the one cake that is good whether or not you add icing. Usually when you bake a cake, you know what type of cake you are going to bake, such as chocolate, lemon, or red velvet. Most cakes have a few general ingredients, but there are some ingredients just for the cake you are baking. Determining the ingredients needed for the cake you wish to become is essential; it allows you to go back and review what is needed. I will suggest some general ingredients; however, as you read the general ingredients, start thinking about other ingredients that you may need for your cake.

We often hear, "She is a product of society." This may be said about certain women who have allowed society to shape them and determine their ingredients, and because of this, they may not have become a good cake. Their ingredients might consist of bad decisions, a lack of education, crime, and a lack of self-identity, self-worth, and support systems. That is why it is very important that you look at your own ingredients and determine them for yourself.

When you bake a cake, the plan is to have a cake you can enjoy looking at and enjoy eating, and you may even want to share the cake with others. So getting the right ingredients to make the cake you are trying to create is vital.

When I was putting together my recipe, some of my ingredients were education, a good support system, finances, sacrifice, employment, a change of mind-set, health, my home environment, and spirituality.

I will share some of my experience with my ingredients for the cake that I was baking.

When I first started out, I was not sure of my ingredients and I was not sure about the cake I was trying to make. My ingredients started out basic, like those of many others in my situation—being a teen mother. The primary goal for many at that time, depending on where and how they were raised, was to graduate from high school. There was not much talk about secondary education; the goal after high school was to get a job. The focus for many was not to go further in education and get into a profession, which for most meant going to college.

So I did what I was supposed to do, which was finish high school. At the time, it was very difficult as a teen mother, but I realized it would be hard to raise a child with no high school education. While I was in the twelfth grade, getting closer to graduation I started thinking about my goal prior to becoming a parent of wanting to go in the US Air Force. That was my initial post–high school goal, because I knew I could not afford to go to college. However, when the day came that I was to be sworn in, I went to the proper location but I could not do it! I was a teen mother, and my son's father had already gone into the US Marines, so that meant I would have to sign my parental rights to my child over to my mother. I could not do that; although my mother was okay with that decision, I was not okay with it. That was my son, and I needed to be home to raise him. That's when I started exploring other avenues so I could care for myself and my child. Secondary education became important to me. You see, I realized that in order for me to have a better life and be able to care for a baby, I needed more education. I started researching careers and decided that health care might be a good avenue in which I could make pretty good money. I decided on a trade school because there was no time for college, which I could not afford anyway. The trade school told me I could apply for a school loan to pay for the course, which was good because I did not have any money to pay for school. I had a baby to care for, and my mother was still providing for me and my child.

I went to trade school and became an EKG technician. The course took nine months. Within weeks after graduation, I found a job. You see, in the beginning of my journey I did not have many ingredients to get to the first product, but the work came later as the product improved. I thought I was done with the product that I had set out to become. I had a good job and was making enough money to provide a life for me and my child. I thought my cake was complete, but there are times when others see that a product can be better. It's like when you bake a cake and the cake comes out tasting good but someone suggests adding icing or strawberries, which makes it even better. That is what happened to me on my journey; this is how I went from just a cake to a pound cake!

I was working as an EKG/telemetry technician in a hospital in Philadelphia, and one of the registered nurses I was working with asked me a question: "Why don't you go to nursing school?" Well, after several conversations with her on how do this—how to add new ingredients that I had no idea about—I began to improve the product. I cut my hours at work and started taking classes at the community college to prepare for nursing school. I was on my way to improving my cake. What I did not know then was that God had placed an angel in my path to help me move to the next level of my life. Within the next year, all the telemetry technicians lost their jobs because of changes the hospital made. I went from working part-time while attending college to being unemployed. Life showed me how baking a cake can be easy, but at times when you are adding ingredients to improve it, the process may get harder before it gets easier.

I graduated from community college in Philadelphia, and it came time for me to start nursing school. I was accepted into various schools, but I chose Roxborough School of Nursing. The nursing school I attended had rules the students needed to follow in order to graduate. We were not allowed to work during certain semesters of school, and we had long hours of schoolwork and clinical work. Hearing the demands and challenges that I was getting ready to face was scary. This is when the other ingredients became important, such as a support system. There is no way I could have attended nursing school without help in caring for my son; again, thank God for Mom! I had to look at my finances, because I could work only a certain amount of hours while in school. I had to learn how to adjust my spending, which was very important. I had to sacrifice things like hanging out with friends, buying new clothing, and getting my hair done, and I had to decide which bills would not be paid and how much and what type of food I could buy. I remember one instructor in college saying, "You may eat tuna fish for a few years, but there will come a day when you can have steak."

In order for me to adjust to my new journey, I set out to change my mind-set. I had to learn to think positively even when things were not good. I had to stay focused no matter what my situation looked like. I had to keep reminding myself that at the end of this journey my life would be even better than it was before.

During this time on my journey, I was faced with an issue regarding the thing people need the most: health. I was diagnosed with fibromyalgia, which is a neuromuscular disorder that causes pain throughout the body. Having this disorder was rough, because I was tired and in pain many days, but I had to keep fighting because I had a cake I was improving. I was also faced with issues from repossession to eviction, but I survived them all. It was a very stressful time, but I found peace and strength by attending church every Sunday. My ingredients may not be your ingredients, but I will tell you that having a recipe was a great plan, because I knew that no matter what, the product I was making would be better than the original one.

Here is a list of some ingredients that you may need for the cake you are baking:

1. Education
2. Support system
3. Financial plan
4. Employment/new employment
5. Changed mind-set
6. Health/being healthy
7. Environment/relationships
8. Spirituality

Once you decide which ingredients are needed, you must then place them in order of importance for you. Let's talk about these ingredients a little.

Education is usually a great ingredient to have in your recipe. There was a time when your high school diploma was enough to get you employed; however, these days there is a greater need to further your education past the high school level. If you have decided education is one of your ingredients, have you taken the time to research what you would like to go to school for? Have you taken the time to research different schools? Do you know the cost of the program/class you want to attend? Do you want a degree or a certificate? Do you know how long it will take to finish the classes or courses? Talking to others in your area of interest will help with this process, and making time to meet with an educational advisor will also help.

A good support system is also a great ingredient to add to your recipe; this tends to depend on your home situation. If you have young children, you may need a support system in place. Having that support system will allow you the needed time for school or time just to collect your thoughts to write and think about the steps and ingredients needed for your new journey. Do you have family and friends who will support you in the journey you have set out on? If so, start discussing with them your plans and how you will need them to assist you. If you don't have a support system in place, start the process of getting one in place; trust me, you will need it. All I can say is, thank God Mom was there while I attended nursing school!

Finances may be an ingredient needed in your recipe. When deciding if this is an ingredient you require, you will need to examine your financial situation. Start by asking yourself some questions. Are your finances in order to start your new journey? Many times when you are looking to make changes in life, finances are part of the process. If your finances are not in order, have you taken the time to meet with a financial planner? Do you have a ledger that helps you to keep track of your spending habits? Knowing your spending habits can be very important when you are looking to make changes in yourself. It is important to know what you are spending your money on each day, week, and month. Yes, I said each day. We often have no idea of the amount of money we are spending on a daily basis. If you take the time to write down what you spend on breakfast, lunch, and dinner—especially if you are buying meals from restaurants—you may be shocked and amazed at the amount of money you are throwing away. So if changes to your finances are going to be among the ingredients to get you to your product, then start paying attention to where your money is going.

A new job or employment may be an ingredient. If so, what have you done to start the process? Do you have a résumé, and if so, have you taken the time to update it? Have you started sending the résumés to potential employers, or are you waiting for the job to knock on your door? Have you visited job search sites? If you were called to a job interview, would you have the right attire? Yes, the right attire—your interview attire is not the same attire that you would wear to the club on Saturday night, ladies; it is not the dress that shows your cleavage or the skirt that is so short that your underwear will say hello if you bend over. Being ready for the interview means having the proper attire so that when that call comes you will be ready.

Mind-set is a very important ingredient for creating a new product. You will need to have a mind-set of being ready for change. There are going to be some changes you like and some you do not; however, mind-set change has to take place in order for you to continue in the direction you are going. When you change your mind, the rest of you will follow; you will witness your mind, body, and spirit working together as one team. I believe that the mind, body, and spirit work together; I have witnessed this happen in accomplishing jobs I wanted done. Having a made-up mind is key. When you encounter a person and his or her mind-set is not right, I bet you that that person probably has a mind, body, and spirit that are broken or not connected in some way. But the good news is that you have the ability to change your mind-set. I dare you to try it out; I guarantee you will see your life start to change.

Health is also a key ingredient. If you are not well, you will not be able to achieve the goals that you have set out to achieve. How is your physical health? In order to start a new journey, you must get your physical body in order. Take the time, if you have not in past few months, and see your physician to get an overall checkup. It is hard to do anything if you physical body is out of order. I know this is an area that many people struggle with, but you need energy for the new you on your journey. If you have no energy or you are always sick, then getting to your promised land might be a difficult task. If you need to start working on your health, consider starting exercising and eating right; this may be the key for you. Getting adequate rest is also needed for your journey. My mother always says to me, "Girl, you sleep too much," but sleep is needed to build a good product. The fact is that on your journey there may be many days when you are not able to sleep as much as you would like to. During my two years of nursing school, sleep was the last thing on my list. There were many days when I only had two hours of sleep before class or clinical work at the hospital. On graduation day my friends asked what I wanted to do, and my reply was "Sleep!" because for those past two years I had missed a lot of it! So when you can sleep, take advantage of it.

How is the environment you live in? How is the temperature in your home? Is it cold, hot or just right? I briefly mentioned this earlier in discussing the temperature of the oven for the cake to come out perfect; however, this principle also applies to the environment you live in. This concept of temperature is related to the environment in your home. Your home environment can play a key role in your process of making changes in your life. Have you ever walked into a person's home and it was warm and inviting, and the people in the home appeared to be pleasant and happy? That's more than likely a home with a good temperature.

If you live in a home environment where there are always negative issues—maybe family members do not coexist well or are unhappy, never saying anything positive—then the temperature in that house is probably very cold, which is not good for growth. Many times, one of the things that may need to change is the temperature of your home. Ask yourself what temperatures you like in your home; most people don't take the time to think about this, but then they wonder why they never reach their goals and dreams. The temperature can be related to relationships in your home. These relationships may be with your children, other family members, friends, or your significant other. If your relationships in your home do not produce growth in you, there may need to be some changes. Most times good things cannot grow when it is too cold or too hot. Think about a cake: will it cook if the oven is too hot or too cold? I like my home just right—neither hot nor cold. I have found though my own trials that I don't grow in a home in which the temperature is not right.

When I realized that the temperature in my home environment was stopping my growth, it was time to make some changes in my home, and it may be time for you do the same. Let me explain what I mean about making changes in your environment to change the temperature so you can grow. Take inventory of who is living in your home. Yes, it may be the people who are residing in your home, it may be that negative mate who wants to argue or not support your dream, or it may be the children who don't want to grow up or who disrespect you while they continue to live in your home without contributing to the "take care of the house fund." So if you are looking to change and grow, make sure to check the temperature in your home. It may be time to do some spring cleaning!

Where do you turn to get inner peace and strength? Spirituality may help you in becoming the product you are trying to become so that you can reach your promised land. Spirituality can help with the balance in your life. Not everyone expresses their spirituality the same, but what I suggest is that you find something that will help you find inner peace. This will help you to become the product you wish to become, because this journey to your promised land is not an easy journey. I am not here to tell you whom to serve or worship, whomever you decide to serve or worship is a matter of personal preference. Meditating, praying, or just closing your eyes to reflect can do wonders for your spiritual being.

So how do you develop a recipe? Think about who you want to become, and then write down all the ingredients needed. For example, since I am a nurse, let's use that as an example. The first thing I did was purchase a notebook and write "Nursing School" on the front. In this book I wrote everything I needed to do to prepare for and finish nursing school. This book is where I kept my ingredients for my recipe during my two years of nursing school.

Now that we have finished reviewing some potential ingredients for your recipe and I have shared a few of mine, I want you to take some time and think about what ingredients you need to either start or complete your cake.

The next step in getting to your promised land is to develop a road map. What is a road map? A road map is a set of directions that lead to a destination. The road map you will create will be the steps and direction you plan on taking to get you to your destination. The road map is like the time frame of baking a cake. The plan of baking a cake usually starts out with a thought: *I want to bake a cake.* That thought then becomes a goal, such as *On Saturday I am going to bake a cake.* Many things we do in life start out with setting goals.

Setting goals is a process in which most people think about what they want to do first. Then the next step of a goal is planning to complete it. What is a goal? Goals are those things that we set out to do and achieve, such as earning a degree, marrying, buying a home, purchasing a car, or traveling the world. Goals usually have a beginning and ending. There are three types a goals: short-term, long-term, and unintentional goals. Your short-term goals most of the time are things you want to achieve within days to months. Your long-term goals are things you want to achieve within three to five years. Unintentional goals are the things that have been in your mind—you know, the things you always talked about doing with others but never got around to doing. These may be goals like skydiving, climbing a mountain, or driving across the coast. They may not be life-changing goals, but just goals pertaining to things in life, which are important as well.

Goals need to be written down, and you need to revisit them either daily or weekly, especially if you have short-term goals.

Try to review long-term goals monthly. One thing I have always done is say thank you to my God when I complete a goal, because I understand that without him I would not meet my goals. I also note the date on which I complete the goal to see if I completed it in the time frame that I wrote down.

There are some rules regarding setting goals. When setting goals, consider these questions: What goals do I want to set? When do I want to achieve this goal? Why do I want to do it? Goals need to measurable, realistic, and flexible. Goals should have a timeline in place. Having a timeline keeps you focused on your goal. Goals are often the reason we get up daily, because we have something to work toward. Do you have goals? Surprisingly enough, that may sound like a stupid question. However, many people do not have goals; they just live life day by day with no purpose. If you find a person with no goals, I will bet that person is an unmotivated, empty person.

Let me ask you a question. What goals do you have other than getting up daily and going to work and paying bills? If those are the only goals you have, then I have to ask, are you really living a productive, fulfilling life? If you have never thought about goals, it's never too late to start.

Your goals become part of your road map. They have a starting point and a destination. You need a road map to take a trip anywhere you are going, whether it's a day trip, a weekend, or a monthlong trip. This destination is your promised land. To get to your promised land, you must map out the directions you want to follow. Again, writing them down will allow you to go back and review to ensure you are on the right road.

Whenever you take a road trip, it is necessary to have a road map or directions, because along the journey there may be detours, road closings, or construction, and having a map and directions accessible makes it easier to find your way back to a road that will lead you to your destination. Let's use MapQuest or a GPS as an example. You type in your starting location and your ending location, and what you get back is several directions, a long route and a short route, and the time it will take you to get to the destination.

Yes, these mapping systems will give you an estimated time frame of how long it will take to reach your destination; however, they do not account for the detours, dead ends, or road construction sites. Of course not all of these obstacles are in the directions, but they could nevertheless cause an increase in the time it takes you to reach your destination. Although these road issues may cause a delay in your travel, you must not allow them to stop or distract you. No matter how hard we try and how closely we watch the road while trying to reach our destination in a timely manner with no road or car issues, things happen along the journey. When you encounter any type of issues during your journey that may cause a delay in your arrival time, don't let it frustrate, discourage, or stop you. Take time to stop, reflect, regroup, and refocus, and then get back on the road. Remember to focus on your destination and not the roadblocks and you will get to your promised land. Know that although you may not be the primary driver in the car, you are in the car, and you will get to your destination if you are holding the map and reading it.

So how do you develop a road map? Creating your road map is all about setting times and goals. Again, I will use my journey to becoming a nurse as an example. This is an abbreviated timeline I made to reach my destination:

- Start community college part-time in fall 1992 to finish with degree in 1994.
- Start nursing school in 1995 to graduate by 1997.

Now take the time to map out your road map to your destination.

I believe everyone who desires to have a purpose and plan for her life should have a recipe and a road map. Although you may have written out the right ingredients and a great road map, there are times when things may go haywire, and as I stated before, you may come up on a roadblock, obstacles, or road closings. When these things happen, you may become frustrated because you have worked so hard on your plans. Whatever you do, don't give up. There may be times you feel like you have been just driving and driving and getting nowhere and you start asking yourself, "What do I do? Should I give up and settle, do I turn this vehicle around and go back to what I know, or do I keep driving?" One thing I do know is that if you keep on driving, you will get to your destination. It may not always happen in the time frame that you mapped out, but you will get there. And if your recipe is not producing the cake you desire, just keep on adding ingredients and letting people sample it; you will soon get to the cake you are aiming to achieve. I promise you that no matter what is going on with your recipe and your road map, whether positive or negative, if you keep being focused, you will make it to your promised land. As H. Stanley Judd noted, "A good plan is like a road map; it shows the final destination and usually the best way to get there."[1]

CHAPTER 2 REFLECTION

List the ingredients you need in order to make or improve your cake.

Are there any obstacles you are facing in relation to your recipe and road map?

What does your road map look like?

Tonya Latney

"And the Lord answered me, and said, write the vision, and make it plain upon tablets, that he may run that readeth it."

—Habakkuk 2:2

PERSONAL REFLECTIONS

CHAPTER 3
The Dream

When you hear the word "dream," what comes to your mind? When I think about the word "dream," I think about desires. Many times throughout our lives, we sit and think about the things we want in life and the things we do in life. What is a dream? Wikipedia defines dreams as "successions of images, ideas, emotions, and sensations that occur involuntarily in the mind during certain stages of sleep." It also states, "Sigmund Freud, who developed the discipline of psychoanalysis, wrote extensively about dream theories and interpretations. He explained dreams are manifestations of our deepest desires and anxieties."

What a dream is may be viewed differently by everyone. Dreams can be a way our minds communicate things to us. Dreaming can be affected by many things, positive and negative, in our lives. Dreaming can keep many people going in life when things get rough, because if you have a dream, then you have a reason to get up and fight every day.

Dreams for some people may be the key that unlocks their future. There are times when I wake up out of a dream and I feel as though my brain was on autopilot, but I wake up with new goals, a new drive, and a new motivation for life. Dreaming can give you the drive and desire to reach your destiny. But what is the next step that needs to take place after you dream? If you are dreaming about something you want or want to do, you need to make it a reality. How do you make a dream a reality? Well, whenever I dream, I feel as though it was placed in me for a reason; I must either have it or do it. I live my life on dreaming because I believe that when you stop dreaming, you stop living, as you are then not looking forward to anything. I believe dreams help connect us with our gifts and reveal our purpose.

It is my belief that in order to have a truly fulfilled life, you must understand that we all have gifts and a purpose. I believe that everyone has a gift in her. Your gift may be revealed at a young age, or it may be revealed later in life. Although you have this gift, you may not know exactly what to do with it.

I believe our gifts are the things we like to do and want to do. When you discover your gift, it will be the thing that you can do without a price; it is the thing that keeps you up at night trying to perfect it. It is my belief that gifts are in us from birth. Your gift in your life is the thing you can do well with no effort or preparation most times, and the thing you like to do anytime. Your gift is the thing you will do for money but also for free because you just love doing it. Most times you don't have to do much planning regarding your gift other than determining how and when to use it. Although you have the gift, it may need some fine tuning and perfecting.

For instance, say you can sing. Perhaps many people noticed that you could sing when you were a child; they may not have seen it as your gift, but rather as something you just could do. There are others gifts people possess: dancing, acting, creating, making people laugh, and speaking life into people.

I did not realize my gift for many years, although I started using my gift very early in life, in elementary school. My gift of helping people solve problems was in me as a child. I definitely did not see this gift as a child, although I was the Dear Abby of my fifth-grade class; I was called Tootsie.

So you see, although I was afraid to speak in front of the class, I was helping from behind the scenes, because everyone wrote letters to Dear Abby. Many of my friends probably don't know that or do not remember that, I am sure. After years of fulfilling many of my goals, my gift was revealed to me. I realized that my gift was to help others. Everything I did as a registered nurse was about helping people; I helped patients and their families. As a wedding planner, I help brides to have a beautiful wedding. My organization, Society of Women Business Owners, has a mission to help women in business to network with other business owners. And now as an author, I hope that my mission will continue in helping someone to birth her gift and find her purpose.

I hope that you reflect on your life so that if you don't know what your gift is, it will be revealed to you. Take some time and think about a thing that you could do all day and night for money or for free. When you find the answer, that is probably your gift.

I have a belief that for some people, your gift is the same as your purpose. For instance, I love talking to people about birthing their dreams. At one point I thought it was something that I just enjoyed doing. I saw it a gift, but I then, over time, I realized it was not just a gift, but my purpose for existence.

Dreams drive us to our destiny in life, which is our promised land.

CHAPTER 3 REFLECTION

What do you dream about?

Do you know your gift?

List two goals you want to achieve this year.

Tonya Latney

"If you can't figure out your purpose, figure out your passion. For your passion will lead you right into your purpose."

—T. D. Jakes

PERSONAL REFLECTIONS

CHAPTER 4
Your Attitude

As you travel your journey to get to your promised land, one of the things you must learn is the power of attitude. Your attitude can take you off your journey, or it can keep you on your journey. Many things will happen on your journey, but the way you react with your attitude will make the difference between winning and losing. As Winston Churchill once said, "Attitude is a little thing that makes a big difference."

The word "attitude" has a great deal of power that many do not understand. A person's attitude can shoot you to the moon or sink you like quicksand. Your attitude is shaped from the time you are born in this world. The culture that you are raised in also shapes your attitude. The first questions that need to be asked are as follows: What is attitude? Do you believe attitude is important? I have heard many people say over the years, "This is my attitude; take or leave it." How far do you think people get in life with this type of attitude? Probably not too far. Attitude is often the way we respond to people and situations around us. Attitude also tells people about who we are.

Attitude is often a behavior learned from one's internal and external environment. Examples of your external environment are your home, your neighborhood, and the state you reside in. Your internal environment is your state of mind. Although attitude is a learned behavior, the great news is that you have the power to control and change it internally and externally.

There are times when a person is unaware of how her attitude is displayed externally. You can display your attitude both consciously and unconsciously. Your attitude is expressed in various manners, from the way you dress to the way you talk and walk. The messages about your attitude are sent from your internal environment to the external environment in these different manners.

For instance, if you were raised in a negative home environment, your attitude may be displayed in a negative manner toward others in your facial expressions. You may walk around not smiling. However, if you have a positive attitude, you may smile most of the time. Your spoken words can convey whether you have a positive or negative attitude. If you have a voice that conveys anger or negativity, that may be a sign of a bad attitude. A pleasant speaking voice, on the other hand, may be a sign of a positive attitude. If you have a negative attitude, you might walk with your head down; but if you have a positive attitude, you might walk with you head up.

Your words and facial expressions are not the only signs of your attitude. The clothing you wear may scream negative attitude. Ladies, this could be clothing that is not meant for your body type. That could mean size or shape; I am sure you know what I mean. If you are not sure if your attire is projecting a negative attitude, ask a friend or family member that you know will tell you the truth. Just be ready, because sometimes the truth really hurts. However, attire is not a deciding factor on attitude, because I have met some well-dressed people with very bad attitudes. There are times when people do not even realize that they are displaying a negative attitude, because they come from either a home or neighborhood environment in which negative attitudes are viewed as normal. Usually they are told by an outside person who is not from their environment that they are displaying a negative attitude.

Fortunately, we can change our attitude. As Katherine Mansfield once noted, "Could we change our attitude, we should not only see life differently, but life itself would come to be different. Life would undergo a change of appearance because we ourselves had undergone a change of attitude." The people, places, and things we encounter can have an impact on our attitude. If you think you need to adjust your attitude a little, you can start by asking yourself some questions. What things can you change to display a positive attitude?

There are many external things that can have an impact on your internal environment, causing a negative attitude. it could be as simple as the music you listen to. How does the music you listen to make you feel—positive or negative? Many of my friends know that I will not, for the most part, listen to love songs. Why? Because I believe it makes you "think," I call it "thinking music." Thinking music tends to make you reminisce about things that have happened in your life, usually relationships. The problem with that is that if those thoughts are negative, they may cause an attitude change. Just say you are listening to a song that makes you start reminiscing about an old relationship. Well, before you know it, you start getting mad, and depending on how bad the situation was, it may affect you so badly that you experience a major attitude change. I don't know one woman who does not have a song that brings back memories of some experience about a past love. I personally enjoy listening to positive music, such as gospel and zen; both keep my attitude positive.

What places are you spending time at? How do they affect your attitude? Your place of employment may cause you to have a bad attitude; if that is the case, maybe it is time to seek new employment. The place where you are living may cause you to have a negative attitude; if that is the case, maybe it is time to seek a new living situation. I have heard many people say they are tired of living in the state they were born and raised in, and this may cause a negative attitude; if that is the case for you, then maybe it is time to move to a new state. If a physical place you are in is a negative environment for you, it is time for you to evaluate the situation and make some moves. The people you associate yourself with can be the cause of a negative attitude; if that is the case, maybe it is time to reevaluate the circle you are in. Start associating yourself with people with positive attitudes. It has been proven that when people think positively, they are more likely to succeed in life, so having a positive attitude no matter what happens will point you toward your promised land. Your attitude connects your mind, body, and spirit. When your attitude is positive, you think positively, you feel good, and your spirit gives off positive energy. Have you ever talked to a person with a negative attitude that gives off negative energy that drains you, leaving you feeling like you need to take a nap after you speak with her?

Your attitude can have an effect on your journey to your promised land. Remember the old saying "Your attitude will determine your altitude in life." What is your altitude in relation to your attitude? Attitude can be just as important as money and your credit score. Think about it; how fast do doors close in your face when you have no money and a bad credit score? Now think about adding a bad attitude on top of both of those. How far do you think you are going to get in life? Where do you want to go in life, and how will your attitude affect your journey?

I never thought attitude was that important. Why? Because attitude is not taught in many homes today. The importance of attitude was once taught, but for some reason over the years it has become a lost life value. There was a time when having a bad or negative attitude was not accepted, but today the most advice many get about attitude is not to give your parents any attitude. But what about giving society attitude?

While you are on your journey to your promised land and you are putting together your recipe and road map, you may need to make some attitude adjustments. Not all attitude adjustment is considered positive or negative; it may need to just be different. On your journey, you need to learn the art of attitude. The art of attitude can be displayed in various ways, as mentioned above. Learning how to adjust your attitude based on where you are going in life is essential. The art of attitude is rooted in knowing how to adjust your attitude based on the altitude that you set.

When people view you, what do your spoken words say about your attitude? Do you speak with confidence about who you are and where you are going on your journey? Does your walk show your attitude as confident, or do you walk as if you are in the dark, trying to find your way? Does your body language convey confidence or confusion?

One of the big challenges I had to deal with was my temper. When my temper flared up, it would cause me to have a bad attitude, which was not a pretty sight. It's not good when people know you for your bad attitude. I had to learn how to take control of my attitude and not let others change it with what they say or do to me.

However, I was not always able to take charge of my attitude. I have experienced many situations on my journey in which I have had to check my attitude. There will be situations in which you cannot allow your old attitude to take control of you. In one situation on the job when I was on my journey to become a registered nurse, a coworker called me a not-so-nice name that started with the letter *B*. At the time, my attitude was positive about where I was going. For a quick second, my external environment changed my internal attitude, as I was about to respond to the negative comment. But from out of nowhere, a coworker intervened and removed me from the negative environment. In that moment, I felt as though God had sent an angel to intervene. I believe that God knew that allowing others to change my attitude was a weakness with me. I truly believe God placed that angel around me that day to help me with my attitude. That angel walked me around and around until my attitude was back on track. If I had responded to that negative external factor, it would have taken me off my journey. You see, I was awarded a scholarship for nursing school, but in order to receive it, I could not have any negative issues at work. I have always believed that angels have been camped around me in my journey, and that day my angel was named Duck. I will always love him for this; he intervened because he knew the journey that I was on. Even though I felt I lost at that time, I really won. Although it is a struggle at times, I have learned not to let people change my attitude. For encouragement along these lines, read these wise words from Charles R. Swindoll: "We cannot change our past ... we cannot change the fact that people will act in a certain way. We cannot change the inevitable. The only thing we can do is play on the one string we have, and that is our attitude. I am convinced that life is 10% what happens to me and 90% of how I react to it. And so it is with you ... we are in charge of our Attitudes."

CHAPTER 4 REFLECTION

What does your attitude say about you?

Think about your altitude based on your attitude. What changes do you think you need to make to your attitude?

Tonya Latney

"Jesus was saying that you can't have a larger life with restricted attitudes."

-Joel Osteen

PERSONAL REFLECTIONS

CHAPTER 5

Trapped

Many people do not see life circumstances as a means of being trapped; however, they can be such a means. There are many people who have never lived a fulfilled life because they have become trapped in the life they were living. There are many things that can cause a person to become trapped. Internal and external factors can cause a person to fall into a trapped cycle. Things such as your paycheck, your environment, and your own mind can trap you. Many people do not see that these factors are trapping them. Although there are many factors that can cause a person to become trapped, they may not always be considered negative things. In fact, many can be very positive, such as a paycheck. However, if there are other things in life that you would like to achieve but you can't because you depend on that paycheck, guess what—you may be trapped! There are some people who do not even realize they are trapped or on a road to becoming trapped!

Many people get trapped in what are known as "generational curses" in our societies. That is, each generation does the same as the generation before them, preventing them from progressing and keeping them in the same poverty mentality. They have a trapped mind-set. How many families do you know that have not changed for generation after generation? This may be a situation where no one in the family is educated past high school. It could be that no one in family moved out of the neighborhood they grew up in. The new generation does not improve from the generation before them. There is no progression in the family, and the family continues the same cycle of mental poverty. Breaking the cycle of generational curses at times can be difficult to do.

From the projects to the promised land

Let me give you an example of a generational cycle. Your mother graduated high school and maybe went to trade school. She moved into her own home in the same neighborhood as her mother. She had dreams of doing other things in life; however, that was delayed because she started having children. She never fulfilled these other dreams because her generational cycle began. Her cycle became one of going to work and coming home to take care of her kids and the house, and before she knew it, that was her life. She began living paycheck-to-paycheck, never reaching her real goals or dreams for her life. Yes, she thought about a recipe, but she never had the time to write it and do it, so as a result she never became the person she wanted to become. Yes, indeed, she became a productive person, but not the one she envisioned herself as. Later in life, her children did the same, none of them ever becoming the person they really wanted to be.

People often don't want to be honest about where they are in life and what they are doing with their life. What happens when this is the case? Their situation never changes. There are things we can do to either stay in that cycle or get out, but we have to start by thinking and seeing reality. If you are reading this and getting mad, then more than likely you are in a generational curse. If you are nodding your head, then you are probably a person who either broke the curse or is in the process of breaking it.

I can reflect back on my own life and can see several ways in which I was trapped, became free, and was trapped again, so I know that this issue of being trapped can be an ongoing thing in your life's journey. Being trapped is not the issue; the issue is how you handle being trapped.

Sometimes you have to sit and reflect back on situations in your life. As I reflect back on the years after I had a baby, while I was still living at home, I realize that it was during that time that I started looking at my environment and asking myself questions about my external and internal environment.

Let me share with you where my journey began. I was raised in the housing projects of Philadelphia in a section of the city called North Philly, which for some people living in the city was not considered a good part of the city to live in. I say "some people" because although it was an area of housing projects, many outsiders that did not live in North Philadelphia did not know that it was a project area. The projects that I was raised in at the time were not viewed negatively, because most people kept them nice inside and out, which is not typical for housing projects. It's funny, because the people who lived there never said, "I live in the projects"; they always said, "I live in Harrison Plaza"—but Harrison Plaza was a housing project. Those of us living in the Harrison Plaza project did not feel that we were living in a project.

As I was finishing this book, I experienced a funny situation. I was working as a home care nurse, and I entered the address of my patient's home on my GPS. As I was arriving at the destination, I saw two high-rise buildings, and as I was driving up the path, I realized that they were projects. I called my mother, laughing, and said to her, "Living in the Harrison projects truly spoiled me, because I feel odd that I have to go into the projects to see a patient." She began to laugh too and said, "Right, right. Chick, you from the projects too." The reality then set in that I had once lived in the same type of high-rise building. As I entered the building, I was still

From the projects to the promised land

laughing as I thought about how the Harrison projects made the people living there "bourgie." I know I am not the only one who thinks this way! Although the projects that I came from were not the typical projects, it was still the projects, and the projects anywhere can cause many to live trapped lives.

When I speak about being trapped in this situation, it has nothing to do with location; instead, it refers to mind-set. I would not change that portion of time in my life if I could, because it helped to shape me into who I am today. I became fearful when I started really looking at my environment. I saw many families living in the same cycle of mental poverty with the mind-set of just getting by. There came a time in my life when I felt that if I did not make changes, I would become trapped too. I started to think about my situation and realized that by staying on the path I was on—having a baby as a teenager—I was setting myself up for the same cycle. I needed to break the cycle. What I came to understand later in life was that there is a lot of stereotyping about people who live in the projects. Many feel that if you live in the projects, you don't want anything out of life, you have no dreams or goals in life, and you have a mentality of poverty. There are some people who believe that everyone in the projects just thinks, *What do I need to do to just get by this week?* Although that is true in some situations, it is not true for everyone. It was not true for me; nor was it true for many others I know who came from the projects. There are quite a few successful people who were raised in the projects.

As my life went on, I began to meet people in different regions. I realized that mental poverty does not only apply to living in the projects. It is not the location that makes you trapped; it is your mind-set. You can live in the biggest house on the highest mountain but have a mind-set of poverty. Your external environment can be where you're living or where you go daily, such as your job. After realizing this, I became very interested in people and how they were trapped. I started people-watching. I know that sounds crazy, but I am telling the truth. I started watching people and listening to their conversations about how they were living and how they felt life was treating them. I did not do this for gossiping purposes but for my own personal growth. There were many times throughout the years I would commute on public transportation, sometimes city to city or state to state. As I did this, I began to observe individuals' facial expressions and postures. During this time, I started wondering, *Are these people happy? Are they doing what they want to do in life, or are they doing what society has told them to do?* I noticed that they dressed in various ways, from suits to uniforms, and I wondered whether they decided on their attire or whether society chose their attire for them. I began to wonder how many people got up daily and hated to put that uniform or suit on.

The first question I want to ask you is, are you trapped in your attire? I know that may sound crazy or far-fetched, but trust me, many people are trapped and forced to put on attire because of life's responsibilities. People may not even realize that they are trapped by their job because of the financial responsibilities in life. They are trapped by the need for the finances that they receive on a weekly or biweekly basis—the paycheck. I do understand how many end up trapped in this cycle, which can be almost the same as a generational curse. It starts for many this way: you are raised to finish high school and get a job, and that is what many do. Then the cycle begins. You get a job so you can get a paycheck, you get a place to live, and life starts. Before you know it, you are trapped by life's responsibilities—getting a paycheck to pay bills, with nothing more in your life. If you are reading this book and this is you, then you need to ask yourself whether you have to work at a job that you are not happy with in order to meet your financial responsibilities. Do you have to stay trapped by your employment? I was once trapped by a paycheck until I was laid off, so I do understand. It was not until I was laid off that I realized that when you are ready for a change, sometimes things like losing a job can be blessings if you are trapped in a situation. So what happens if you lose your job? Most times we look at it in a negative manner, but it could be the thing that releases you from the situation and mind-set that have you trapped.

As I stated in the beginning, being trapped is not always a negative situation; it can be a positive situation. Let me share my positive situation of being trapped. As I discussed a little earlier I was working as telemetry technician in a Philadelphia hospital. I had been in that position for many years, I was happy, I was making a decent salary, and I was pleased with the attire that I needed to wear to do the job. However, once I decided that I wanted to attend nursing school, I began to feel trapped by my job. I felt trapped because I needed the paycheck. I would think daily about what I could do to still get a paycheck and go to school. Again, as I stated before, you cannot work even part-time while attending most nursing schools, so I was feeling really trapped. I was starting to feel what most people feel when going to jobs they don't wish to go to because of other goals they wish to achieve. I was very unhappy and frustrated, but then I was freed when I was laid off. That change allowed me to reach my goal of becoming a registered nurse, or RN. Hooray! I worked many years as a happy nurse again, making a good living, only to find that I was trapped again several years later! This time it was not a goal or a dream that I wanted to achieve; instead I wanted to use my gift, the reason I believe I was placed here on earth. Once my gift was revealed to me, I began to feel trapped by my attire again. Every time I had to wear a pair of scrubs, I would get mad, because I knew that was not the only attire I was supposed to be wearing. However, although I hated putting on that nurse attire, I did not see it as a negative issue or feel trapped; in fact, I loved being a nurse. I was just ready to move to the next level in my life. I had a new promised land awaiting my arrival! So being trapped for me at different times has been negative and positive. As you can see, we can become trapped in various ways throughout life.

I don't know what situation you are facing, but I do know that as women we are faced with many situations that cause us to feel trapped on our journey at times. Just having children and being married can cause us to feel trapped. Being married and having children are both rewarding and joyful events, but at times it means putting on that attire you do not want to put on and going into a physical environment you do not wish to be in. You may feel trapped physically, but do not let your mind become trapped.

I have come across many people who really do not understand why they are not happy and find themselves always complaining about things in life. The problem is usually that they have become trapped in their own life. They feel like prisoners; they are existing but not living.

Being a nurse working with the elderly population has afforded me the opportunity to meet people who have lived fulfilling and good lives. I was once working as a nursing supervisor, and I was getting reports from another supervisor. An angry patient came to us complaining about her care nurse, and her comment to us was "All I want is a towel." The nurse and I looked at each other after the resident left, and we laughed. I said, "I hope that at the end of my days, all I desire is a towel." The point I am making is that you should not get trapped in life and not live the life you desire for yourself; nor should you let society dictate what attire you wear.

There are many people who want to do other things, such as going back to school for a degree, starting their own business, or even relocating to another state, but they feel trapped. The goal is to learn how to free yourself so you can make it to your promised land. It all leads back to your road map and recipe. How many times have you been driving, got lost, and felt as though you were going in a circle, but eventually you got back on the right road to your destination? Well, this is no different. You may feel trapped, but if you start focusing on your destination and not your situation, then you will make it to your promised land.

To start making changes to becoming free, you need to start looking at your external environment. Where do you live? Is it a positive or negative environment? Is this keeping you trapped? Where do you work? Is this keeping you trapped? Who are the people you share your space and time with? Are they keeping your trapped? What things are you doing to keep yourself trapped?

I know it is probably easy to think about all the external factors that may be keeping you trapped, but I am sorry to say that there is no—I repeat, no—external factor that can keep you trapped. The only thing that will ever keep you trapped is you and how you think.

Yes, your internal environment, your mind-set, is what will dictate your life. You may be trapped, but if you change your mind-set, you can become free.

Getting free really does not start with external factors; it starts internally, with your mind-set. As long as you are thinking in a trapped way, you will stay trapped. I dare you to start looking at your situation in a positive manner. Begin surrounding yourself with people who do not feel trapped. When you start internalizing who you want to be and where you want to go, watch how things start changing for you. Remember, it starts with the mind.

If you could change your attire, how would you dress? If the attire you would like to wear is different from what you are wearing, start making plans to change that attire.

Reflect back on the chapters about your dreams, gifts, and goals, and think about what is inside of you.

CHAPTER 5 REFLECTION

Can you relate to any type of generational cycle?

What does "trapped" mean to you?

Do you feel trapped by your attire or by the paycheck you are receiving?

"Three Rules of Life … 1: Your time is limited, so don't waste it living someone else's life. 2: Don't be trapped by dogma—which is living with the results of other people's thinking. Don't let the noise of others' opinions drown out your own inner voice. 3: Have the courage to follow your heart and intuition—they somehow already know what you truly want to become."

—Steve Jobs

PERSONAL REFLECTIONS

CHAPTER 6
Keep It Moving

Keep it moving! This is my advice in any situation, no matter the good, bad, or ugly. There are many events and distractions in life that can cause people to stop following the course they are traveling. The problem is not the events and distractions; it is how we respond to those events and distractions. At times these events and distractions in our lives can knock us off the course to our destiny. However, you cannot allow that to happen. The key is to learn how to handle them and get back on the road to your destination. There are some events and distractions we can control, and there are many we can't. The important thing is not to allow them to keep you off your road to your destination. Should you take a moment to absorb what has happened to you? Yes, but get back on track and keep it moving, because after all, you made a decision, a recipe, and a road map, and you need to stay the course to reach your promised land. When these events or distractions happen, do what you need to do to get over them. Cry, yell, scream, or kick; do one or do them all, and then keep it moving! I had to do all of them at one time or another on my road to my destination, but after that I got back on track, and that is what you will need to do.

I see life events and distractions as traffic lights and traffic signs. There are stop signs, yield signs, merge signs, etc., but remember that when we come to one of these signs, we may have to stop for a moment, but we get to move again. Let's look at the traffic light as an example. Red tells us to stop, and yellow tells us to slow down, but green, which tells us to go, always follows. On your journey, you will encounter traffic lights and signs; they are necessary for you to reach your promised land. The events and distractions you encounter in reaching your destiny are all part of the plan; no one arrives at her promised land without them. They are necessary evils that are strategically placed to give us strength for the journey.

Problems can occur when you do not handle life events and distractions in a smart and careful manner. For example, your plan and destination can be changed to someone else's plan rather than your own. Life events and distractions will happen to all of us. I have had my share; trust me. But I live what I am telling you, and that is to keep it moving!

Some of the life events and distractions that a person can encounter while on her journey are job loss, financial issues, problems with children, homelessness, marriage/relationship issues, health issues, abuse, drug/alcohol addiction, unplanned pregnancy, and death.

Let us talk about some of these issues.

Job Loss

I remember losing a job, but guess what—it was all part of the plan to get me to my promised land. You may lose your job and find that what you think is a setback is actually a setup that pushes you closer to your promised land.

I received the call that many fear from their employer these days because of what is going on with the economy. The call I received at home on my day off explained that I needed to come in for a mandatory meeting. When I arrived at my place of employment, I found a group of my coworkers sitting in a room around a large conference table. A person from management entered the room, thanked us for being employees at the hospital, and told us our services were no longer needed. I was laid off! I remember going home after the meeting and thinking about what I was going to do. I started thinking the worst, which of course caused me to start crying. When I finally collected myself, I took the next step in the process and applied for unemployment. To my surprise, my unemployment check amounted to a little less than my paycheck. This allowed me to attend college full-time, so what I initially saw as a setback was really a setup for me to get closer to my promised land. I know that may not be the case for everyone, but if this does happen to you, although it may be scary, try to think about the positive in it.

Remember, when one door closes, there will be another door for you to open and walk through. The funny thing (although it is not a time to laugh when job loss is involved) is that this may be the time when your promised land is revealed to you. Not having a job can give you the time to do some research or explore things that you would not have time to do while working. We often can't see the positive. In the beginning, all we see and think is negative until the smoke clears, but when the smoke clears—and it will clear—what should you do? Keep it moving.

I was mentoring a young lady that wanted to start her own business. At the time I met her she was employed but not doing what she really wanted to do. She had other plans for her promised land. One day she was fired from her job and she called me. I gave her a thirty-day challenge to change her direction and focus on her promised land. After thirty days she had her own business going and never looked back. Sometimes losing a job can be a blessing, but many times we don't see it until later. So if you encounter a job loss, take a moment to breathe and think. As I always tell people when they are fired, send your employer a thank-you letter and keep it moving, because more than likely your employer is helping you get closer to your promised land.

Financial Hardship

This seemed to be the hardest thing for me to conquer and master on my way to my promised land. Just know that everything works together, even though it may not seem that way while you are on your journey. You have made your recipe and road map, and yes, finances may play a part getting you to your promised land. We all need finances to take care of our daily and monthly living expenses, but there are times when you have goals and those extra finances are not there. Many people have big dreams but little money; just know that money is not always the answer to getting you to your promised land. Having drive and desire can open many financial doors for you. Your drive and desire can be more valuable than a million dollars. Money with no purpose or plan will get you nowhere but broke again. So as you set out on your journey, keep it moving. Even if you don't see the financial help, trust me—it will come.

Unplanned Pregnancy

It's really sad to say that many people don't really plan to have children, but sometimes it just happens. I find that it's not important how it happened to me, because guess what—it happened. Having children can knock you off course for a moment, but don't let it be an excuse for why you have not gotten to your promised land. You may need to take time and rewrite your recipe and road map to get to your promised land, but it can be done. I had a baby at sixteen; it was not easy, but I did it. So really there is no excuse. Find your support system, make a plan, and keep it moving.

Marriage

Marriage can be challenging if you do not have a person by your side that will be a true helpmate on your journey to your promised land. The union of marriage is difficult in itself. Marriages are often like two people in the kitchen at the same time, trying to bake a cake with ingredients all over the place and no order. The problem in many marriages is that there is an art to it that many have not mastered. If you are working on your recipe and your road map to get you to your promised land, you need support from your mate; that should be one of the ingredients in your recipe. If this is your situation, do not let martial problems take you off your road. Your promised land may be connected to self-fulfillment, and if you are not happy with who you are, then you will not have a happy marriage. Some people feel that you should reach this destination before getting married. The bottom line is, whatever the issues in your marriage are, try to work them out, but do not let these issues stop you from reaching your promised land. You must deal with your marital issues. If things work out, great, but if they don't, do what you need to do to get yourself back on track, and keep it moving.

Homelessness

Just because you have a place to lay your head does not mean you have a home. Home is a place of peace away from the chaotic outside world. When you are trying to work on the recipe of your life, you need to have peace so you can think. You are about to become a great product, and you need to write your recipe and road map. You may be in a situation where you don't have a home. If that is the case, you need to find a place of peace. Finding a place of peace will allow you time to work on your recipe and road map. This place of peace may be a library or the local park. Dedicate an hour or two once a week to being in this place. If you currently do not have a home, just remember not to let your situation be a negative thought. Deal with it, and just remember to keep it moving!

Loss of a Loved One

I have never experienced the loss of a loved one in my own family that caused me to stop my journey to my promised land. But I did experience the loss of a friend who was very near and dear to me; she happened to be one of my bosses. Juanita, God bless you! During the time of my loss, I was working on my recipe of becoming a registered nurse. My boss was a motivator and positive person; she really looked out for me, and when she passed, it hurt me dearly, but she became a part of my recipe. I knew my boss wanted me to become a nurse, so although I was hurt, I had to keep it moving, I believe that if she could have said anything to me after passing, that is what she would have told me to do. I will never forget her, because she is part of my recipe for the product that I became. There is a grieving process that most of us have to go through when we have lost a loved one. Yes, you have to go through the process to heal yourself mentally. After you go through the grieving process, don't let your loss stop your journey to the promised land. Instead, add the person you lost to your recipe, because when you add that person, he or she will always be an ingredient within you. If the person you lost could talk to you, he or she would probably say, "Keep it moving and make me proud."

Abuse

Many people have suffered abuse, both physical and mental, on many different levels in their lives. Being a victim of abuse can take you off your course in life. One of the key factors in dealing with abuse is to first be able to admit to yourself that you are being abused. Once you admit that you are a victim of abuse, then the healing can begin. There is no one reason why someone is abused, but the key is to get out of the abusive relationship and to understand that you are worthy of better than that. The problem that I have seen with abuse victims it that it is hard to break the cycle of abuse, meaning that even though such victims may get out of the situation, they continue to talk about it. Yes, they do need to talk about what they have been through. They may choose the path of a professional, such as a physician or psychologist, or maybe just family and friends. If you are a victim of abuse, choose to deal with it and move on, no matter what path you are on. Don't keep reliving it by holding on to it, unless you plan on using it in a positive way by discussing it to help other people who are being abused or were abused in the past. If that's not the case, then move past the experience. Move on by forgiving yourself and then forgiving your abuser. And then keep it moving.

Health

During the time I was in nursing school, I began to get extremely tired and started experiencing pain in my joints. I was diagnosed with fibromyalgia. Fibromyalgia is a disorder that causes a person to experience fatigue and pain all over his or her body. This disorder can debilitate a person. Many individuals who are diagnosed with this disorder are not able to work and experience decreased quality of life because of the pain and fatigue. Dealing with this disorder was very difficult for me because I was constantly tired and in pain, but I learned to use mind over matter to control the pain and fatigue. I was not about to let this disorder win! I still fight with this today; some days it is a real challenge to do all the things that I desire to do, but I just tell my body that we are not going to let the disorder win. So if you are suffering from any health issues that are not life threatening, tell those issues that they are not going to win, and keep it moving. (As a registered nurse I do understand that there are some diseases and disorders that are more challenging to deal with than others; I am not speaking of those, although everyone handles diseases and disorders differently.)

Loss of Yourself

Just as I was finishing this book, I had to deal with this issue. There are times when you are so busy helping others and trying to do right by everyone that the one person you can lose is yourself. If you have ever lost yourself, then you know it can be a painful event in your life. It can leave you feeling tired and having thoughts of no longer wanting to exist. I am not saying you want to commit suicide; it's a feeling of wanting to just disappear. This is not something that all can relate to, and I hope that you never have this feeling. It is a feeling similar to being in a boxing match and thinking, *Do I throw in the towel to say I've had enough?* When I got to this point, it took a lot of soul-searching. I had to search my being to find the reason I am here—my assignment and purpose. For a brief moment I was lost, but God quickly reminded me that I am here on an assignment and this life is not about me alone. I cried some days, and the pain I felt in my stomach was one that I cannot explain except to say that it felt like fire! So while caring for others, make sure you are not giving so much that you lose you. It was hard for me to digest that I had lost myself. I thought I was taking care of me, and I thought I was protecting my mind and my heart, but somehow the enemy got in and almost aborted my mission to my promised land. But I got back in line with my mission and said to myself, "I've got to keep it moving!"

Women often make excuses for why they have not reached their goals because of life events. I know this may be a wake-up call for some, and it may sound a little harsh, but ladies, you need to learn how to keep it moving! Be very careful what you do, say, and think when you encounter life events or distractions; the goal is to deal with them in a positive manner and keep it moving!

Again, when you encounter life events, you may need to seek a professional, such as a psychologist, physician, or counselor from your place of worship. Whatever path you choose, get the help you need; don't let your past ruin your future. It is time to refocus on your dreams and goals. The dreams and goals in you are going to take you to your promised land.

And once again I say, keep it moving.

CHAPTER 6 REFLECTION

Are you facing any life events that may cause you to not make it to your promised land?

What does "keep it moving" mean to you?

Tonya Latney

"Weeping may stay for the night, but rejoicing comes in the morning."

—Psalm 30:4–6

PERSONAL REFLECTIONS

CHAPTER 7
Season, Reason, Lifetime

People come into your life for a reason, a season or a lifetime.
When you figure out which one it is,
you will know what to do for each person.
When someone is in your life for a REASON,
it is usually to meet a need you have expressed.
They have come to assist you through a difficulty;
to provide you with guidance and support;
to aid you physically, emotionally or spiritually.
They may seem like a godsend, and they are.
They are there for the reason you need them to be.
Then, without any wrongdoing on your part or at an inconvenient time,
this person will say or do something to bring the relationship to an end.
Sometimes they die. Sometimes they walk away.
Sometimes they act up and force you to take a stand.
What we must realize is that our need has been met,
our desire fulfilled; their work is done.
The prayer you sent up has been answered and now it is time to move on.
Some people come into your life for a SEASON,
because your turn has come to share, grow or learn.
They bring you an experience of peace or make you laugh.
They may teach you something you have never done.
They usually give you an unbelievable amount of joy.
Believe it. It is real. But only for a season.
LIFETIME relationships teach you lifetime lessons;
things you must build upon in order to have a solid emotional foundation.

> *Your job is to accept the lesson, love the person,*
> *and put what you have learned to use in all other relationships and areas of your life.*
> *It is said that love is blind but friendship is clairvoyant.*
>
> —Unknown

As you go through this journey of life on your way to your promised land, one of the factors that will change is the people you encounter. You are going to find that people are in your life for a season, a reason, or a lifetime. It has been my experience that as you travel on your journey, people will be placed in your life's path to give you a life test, teach you a life lesson, or give you a key to open a another door in your life. I have found that many people enter my life and also leave it, and I have learned that some people must go because they were there for a season or maybe a reason. This has been most challenging for me regarding people who were brought into my life for a test; I had to fail the same test multiple times to realize why those people had been placed in my life.

The challenge with people entering your life is that you have to really pay attention to the signs they show you. These signs will usually reveal why these people have been placed in your life. The changes you will encounter with people in life are like the seasons. Growing up on the East Coast in Philadelphia, I was used to the different seasons: winter, spring, summer, and fall. I knew that I had a certain amount of time to either enjoy or endure each season. Depending on the times of my life's journey, the seasons did not affect me much in a positive or a negative way. As a child I enjoyed winter because that meant school might close and we could play in the snow all day. During the summer months there was no school, and again we could play outside all day. However, in my adult years these changes started to affect me in different ways. During the fall I would start to get sad because winter was coming, and to me winter meant the snow was coming and it would soon be gloomy and cold, which was very depressing to me. But soon spring would come and I could feel the sadness lifting; the trees would become green and blossom, preparing for the summer, when it would be bright and sunny. Many people do not like the changes the seasons bring—I am on the top of the list. But no matter how much we may not like the changes in the seasons, they will come—depending on where you live in the world. If you live where the changing seasons are not a concern … lucky you!

The same principle applies to other things in our lives, such as the relationships we have with people. From the time we enter elementary school as children, when we encounter new friends we think they will be our friends for life and they will always be there. However, just as there are the seasons of the year, we have seasons with friends. Somewhere on our journeys we start losing friends and gaining new ones. Most times we do not really understand why that happens. I have heard comments from many people when they are going through what I call a "change of season." Their friends are not calling or coming around, and they say things like "If they don't call, I am not calling" and "I don't know why they didn't show up." This probably indicates a change in seasons. When we learn that people are in our lives for a reason, a season, or a lifetime, I think we gain a better understanding of the changes that one must encounter in this journey of life, and we learn not to take it so personally.

Losing friends on your journey can be painful at times, depending on the situation or circumstances, but understanding that they may have only been there for a season or reason is important for you to understand. There will be things that happen with friends during your journey that you will not understand. There are going to be many people you encounter that will come and go on your way to your promised land. Meeting people is part of the process on your journey. Some relationships are just setups for you to encounter new relationships. I had a patient that I really became attached to. I looked forward to seeing her daily as she recovered from a fall in which she suffered a few fractures. She and I had great conversations. In one of our conversations I told her that I lived somewhat bicoastally between Philadelphia and Las Vegas. She mentioned that she had a family member that also lived in Las Vegas and she thought it would be great for us to meet. She began making arrangements for her cousin and me to meet on my next trip to Las Vegas. I went to Vegas and met her cousin; we immediately bonded because we had so much in common with our lives. The funny thing about this was my patient had never met her cousin in person. Within the next year or so, my patient passed away. I was saddened because she was gone and because I was unable to go to her homegoing service because I was away. Her cousin said to me, "Don't be sad. Her purpose for meeting you was fulfilled; she allowed us to meet." When I sat and thought about it, I realized that she was absolutely right; she was placed in my life for that short season, and the reason was so I could meet what I believe to be a great lifetime friend.

Seasons are all about change. Seasons often dictate our behavior; for example, if it's raining, there are some people who feel tired, and if it is sunny, many are ready to get out and enjoy the day. Those of us who live in areas of the world with different seasons know how to prepare for change. When winter is coming, we put away summer clothing. We learn to adjust our daily lives based on the changes that come with each season.

When we talk about seasons, we are really talking about adjusting to changes at set times. This really is no different when people come into your life for a season. The problem is that we assume when we meet people that they will be there for a lifetime; that's usually the first mistake many of us make. As people, we go through many seasons from our birth until our death. If you were to talk to a person who is one hundred years old, he or she could probably tell you about many seasons and all the people he or she encountered in his or her lifetime. I believe that just as we make changes for the yearly seasons, we need to make changes for the seasons in our lives that we will encounter with people. The other mistake I believe many of us make is trying to keep season people around for a lifetime, and then when we are faced with the reality that they were just there for a season of our life, we feel hurt and betrayed. Many times its our own fault, because if we learn to listen to and watch what people say and do, just as we watch the seasons change, we can avoid those hurtful feelings in the end.

Just as some people are in your life for a season, they are often placed there for a reason. The reason could be positive or negative. I have found many times that people teach me something about life or myself and then leave; their reason for the encounter is fulfilled, and so that season is done. When you encounter people during a change in season and they cross you or mistreat you, don't be quick to get mad. Ask yourself, "What am I supposed to learn from that person?"

Let me share a season event that happened to me. I met a woman during a change in one of my seasons. For years my cousin had been saying to me, "You tell people too much information about you." I never felt I needed to hide what was going on in my life. Well, needless to say, this woman tried to use my words to hurt me. Yes, I was mad and hurt for a minute, but after I had time to reflect on why she had been placed in my life, I realized that she had been there for a season and a reason; her time was up, so she was no longer part of my life. She was there to help me stop telling people more than they need to know, because not everybody can handle the journey you are on in life. So start paying attention to the people in your life, and as you are on your journey to your promised land, just know that some are there for a season or a reason. If you truly understand this principle on your journey, then when things happen, whether positive or negative, and those people exit your life, just know that they were put in your life to fulfill a purpose. When that purpose has been fulfilled, they are done. This applies to you as a friend to others as well. I have encountered many individuals for whom I was there for just a season or reason. Some people are puzzled when they can't figure out why they were there and now they are gone. We begin to ask ourselves why, but no answer is revealed quickly. What purpose did they play? What was the reason? There are times when that answer may not come until later.

Some are there for a season and a reason, but many will be there for a lifetime. How many lifetime people do you have in your life? This does not include family; they are there whether you want them there or not. Most of us meet our lifetime friends early in life; I met many of mine between age five and age twenty-five, but you can meet lifetime friends later in life as well. Most of the people whom I met during those years are still my friends today; I consider them lifetime friends. We may not talk daily, but when we do talk, it seems as though we talked yesterday. We may not talk for days, weeks, or months, but they are only a phone call away. Lifetime people do not leave when the seasons in your life change, and they are not there for one reason. Lifetime people are there for you when seasons change in your life. Lifetime people have no real reason for being in your life other than that they just love you.

LIFETIME PEOPLE

Love you no matter what

Inform you of your rights and wrongs

Forgive you

Express excitement about good things that happen for you

Trust you

Improve or inspire you

Motivate you

Empower you

When you have lifetime people, you always feel connected and close, regardless of the time, distance, or location.

Just take some time and think about the people who are in your life. Ask yourself whether they are there for a season, a reason, or a lifetime.

As I continue to journey toward my promised land, most of the time it is challenging and exciting to know and understand the principle of season, reason, and lifetime with the people I encounter. This principle has helped me to grow as a person. Getting to your promised land is like going up a staircase and finding that at each landing there is a door you must go through, but you need a key. The people you encounter on your way up will be in your life for a season, a reason, or a lifetime. The key that you need to help get to your promised land is in another person; that is why I find it exciting to meet people on my journey. Just as I believe I am holding a key for someone, I believe that there is someone holding a key for me. As my seasons change and I encounter new people for different reasons, I wonder what they have for me—a test, a lesson, or a key.

CHAPTER 7 REFLECTION

What lessons have you learned from people?

What tests have you been given? Did you pass or fail?

How many lifetime friends do you have?

From the projects to the promised land

"People always come into your life for a reason, a season and a lifetime. When you figure out which it is, you know exactly what to do."

—Brian A. "Drew" Chalker

PERSONAL REFLECTIONS

CHAPTER 8
Success

From the projects to the promised land

Success can be determined and defined differently by different people. To me, success has nothing to do with my bank account but everything to do with my journey and freedom. Freedom, to me, is success. On my journey, my goal is freedom—freedom from someone telling me how many days I can be sick, how many days I use for vacation, and how much money I can make in two weeks, one month, or one year. Freedom to me means living in whatever state I wish to live in week to week or month to month. Freedom for me is working when and as much as I want to, or maybe not at all. When I have reached those goals, then I will feel I have reached success in my life. I believe in the words of Christopher Morley: "There is only one success—to be able to spend your life in your own way."[2]

Would you consider yourself successful if your bank account was empty and you were living paycheck to paycheck, but you were doing what you wanted to do daily? Many people link success to wealth, but is there really a difference? As Franklin D. Roosevelt said, "Happiness is not in the mere possession of money; it lies in the joy of achievement, in the thrill of creative effort."[3]

When you start putting together a recipe and road map, how will you view success? Will success be an ingredient or a final destination for you? There are so many avenues to what one considers success: career, health, spirituality, emotion, and maybe finances. As Chin Ning Chu put it, "A successful life is one that is lived through understanding and pursuing one's own path, not chasing after the dreams of others."[4]

I found it interesting that when I asked most people what

success meant to them, they had to pause and think for a minute. I believe this is because most people don't look at life from a standpoint of success but rather from a survival perspective. Many people today are in survival mode, thinking about where the next meal is coming from and what they have to do with their next paycheck. Yes, we do need to have a survival mode of thinking, but we also need to have a successful mind-set. If one starts to have a successful way of thinking, then I believe that someday that person will not have a total survival mode of thinking. For me success and a survival mode of thinking go hand in hand. Many of us are taught that we must learn how to survive, but very few of us are taught how to become successful. How many people around you are in survival mode only, and how many people do you know consider themselves to be successful? If you have more survival mode people around you than successful people, and your goal is to be successful, it may be a good time to enter a new circle of people who think about being successful.

In order to be successful, you have to first define what success means to you. Once you have decided what it is, then you can start working toward it. Charles Lindbergh had this to say on the issue: "Success is not measured by what a man accomplishes, but by the opposition he has encountered and the courage with which he has maintained the struggle against overwhelming odds."[5]

What I have found while on my journey to my promised land is that the success I was shooting for came with a price. When I finally defined what success meant to me, I realized it was something that was not given to a person but something I had to plan. The areas of success on my journey did not come easily. I live by the three Ps: push, pain, and pray. For all the success that I have gained thus far, I had to push though the opposition and problems I faced. I had to endure the pains of growth that I worked on obtaining, just as a woman in labor endures some level of pain to bear her blessing just before the delivery. I had to pray to keep my strength amid my struggle of wanting and doing better. So my success came with a hefty price.

After all the research I have conducted and all the speaking I have done with different people about what success means, I don't feel success is something that can be defined by one person. I believe success is what you feel it is to you.

I love this success quote:

> To laugh often and much;
> To appreciate beauty, to find the best in others;
> To leave the world a bit better, whether by a healthy child, a garden patch or a redeemed social condition;
> To know even one life has breathed easier because you have lived.[6]
>
> —Bessie Stanley

CHAPTER 8 REFLECTION

What does success mean to you?

What things must you do to obtain success?

What is your goal—success, wealth, or both?

From the projects to the promised land

"Success is not the key to happiness. Happiness is the key to success. If you love what you are doing, you will be successful."

—Albert Schweitzer

PERSONAL REFLECTIONS

CHAPTER 9

Staying Beautiful

A Woman's Beauty
Is not determined by a man
Her beauty can be found in her grace
A woman's beauty is in her heart
Her beauty is her art
—Ms. J Star

Your journey to your promised land will take motivation, dedication, and focus, but you can stay beautiful on the journey. This journey can make you feel run down and ugly at times. Many days you may not feel like doing your hair, putting on makeup, or putting on your best attire (or maybe any attire at all). This journey at times may even cause you to lose sleep or get restless sleep. You may find yourself working late at night and snacking on unhealthy treats, which can cause weight gain. If you start doing any of these things while on your journey, it can affect your beauty inside and out. If you start feeling tired mentally, it will often be reflected in your physical appearance. Taking care of yourself physically, mentally, and emotionally is one of the most important things you can do for yourself while on your journey.

This journey that you have set out to achieve can be hard, but it can be done, and you can stay beautiful and youthful while on the journey. I started my journey at fifteen, and at forty-three I still feel beautiful inside and out. While on this journey, yes, I have gained several pounds, but I am daily very mindful about my beauty. I am not speaking about beauty from only a physical perspective, but also how I feel mentally. There is a saying that goes, "You do not have to look like you feel or what you are going through." Just because you are having a hard time does not mean you have to look as though you are having a hard time.

How do you stay beautiful and youthful while on your journey? When you put together your recipe, one of the ingredients needed is the knowledge of how to take care of yourself mentally and physically, because if you are not healthy, you cannot enjoy your journey, and you may not even finish the journey.

What does taking care yourself mean? It means keeping a plan of how you intend to take care of yourself on this journey. Some of these plans may mean exercising or doing some type of activity that keeps you moving. You may not be able to afford the gym, but the outside is free; take a walk, or maybe just find some steps to run up. I will tell you that I am not one for exercising, but I do try to engage in some type of physical activity, such as walking on my treadmill in my home and/or swimming occasionally. However, I do have other things that I do to ensure that I am taking care of myself inside and outside. I enjoy frequent massages and foot detoxification. Both of these help me to rid my body of negative toxins, which I believe helps my inner and outer beauty.

Diet is also an important factor for your beauty. Eating right gives your body the proper nutrients and energy it requires to stay healthy and beautiful on your journey. Getting the proper rest will also help your beauty. Proper rest is called "beauty sleep" for a reason. I love to sleep. There are days when I work hard, and there are days when I sleep hard. Your body needs rest; if you are tired, you cannot think clearly. Because of this, I make sure I make time to sleep. Learn to take a "me day." Start the day by getting dressed up, and then go out and pamper yourself. This "me day" may be used to go shopping and buy yourself something nice, or it may be used to get your hair done, get a pedicure or manicure or maybe a facial, or just to go see a movie and have dinner. Take some time and just do nothing; I myself love nothing days—days when I just wake up and have no plan for the day. I like sitting outside and just enjoying nature, maybe eating a Rita's Water Ice. The goal is to learn to have balance; you will need it on your journey to your promised land.

When you feel beautiful, you act beautiful and your body feels good. When you feel good, you are able to focus. Being focused will get you to your promised land.

> Beautiful
> Not only because of the curve of my hips
> Or the shape of my body
> I am beautiful because I want to be
> I am beautiful because God made me that way[7]
>
> —Candice George

CHAPTER 9 REFLECTION

What does "beautiful" mean to you?

Do you feel beautiful?

How do you keep yourself beautiful?

From the projects to the promised land

"Beloved, I wish above all things that thou mayest prosper and be in health, even as thy soul prospereth."

—3 John 1:2

PERSONAL REFLECTIONS

CHAPTER 10

The Promised Land

How do you know you have made it to the Promised Land? The only person who will ever know is you. The Promised Land is a self-evaluating tool. As I said in the beginning of the book, everyone has a different promised land, and each person knows what her own promised land looks and feels like.

Have you ever heard of Abraham Maslow's hierarchy of needs?

Abraham Maslow created a pyramid that represents the relative amounts of basic needs and more complex needs. This hierarchy of needs represents the various needs that usually motivate people. Maslow writes, "At the peak of this hierarchy is self-actualization. The hierarchy suggests that when the other needs at the base of the pyramid have been met, the individual can then focus their attention on this pinnacle need. Self-actualization is described as ' … the desire for self-fulfillment, namely, to the tendency for him to become actualized in what he is potentially.'"[8]

MASLOW'S EIGHT LEVEL HIERARCHY OF NEEDS

Level 1

Biological and Physiological needs - air, food, drink, shelter, warmth, sex, sleep, etc.

Level 2

Safety needs - protection from elements, security, order, law, limits, stability, etc.

Level 3

Belongingness and Love needs - work group, family, affection, relationships, etc.

Level 4

Esteem needs - self-esteem, achievement, mastery, independence, status, dominance, prestige, managerial responsibility, etc.

Level 5

Cognitive needs - knowledge, meaning, etc.

Level 6

Aesthetic needs - appreciation and search for beauty, balance, form, etc.

Level 7

Self-Actualization needs - realizing personal potential, self-fulfillment, seeking personal growth and peak experiences.

Level 8

Transcendence needs - helping others to achieve self actualization.

http://www.businessballs.com/maslow.htm

The sad part of looking at the pyramid is that there are only a few people who ever reach the pinnacle. "That so few people reach this level of motivation," Maslow writes (he considered each need to be a motivator), "is unfortunate."

From the projects to the promised land

I believe that all people who have breath in their lungs should have a life that feels like their promised land. The saddest thing that I experience on a day-to-day basis is unhappy people. If you are not happy, take some time for yourself and write or rewrite a recipe for yourself. You deserve to get to your promised land.

You have to envision your promised land; you have to see it as if it exists! You have to ask yourself, "Do I want to exist, or do I want to make it to my promised land?"

I hear people say that it is too late to start on the road to their promised land; well, I beg to differ. I don't think it is ever too late to reach for your promised land. Reaching your promised land is about self-fulfillment. Think about the amount of people who never reach that goal of self-fulfillment. Do you want to be in that crowd? If you are not living the life that will get you to your promised land, please start today with a recipe and start your new journey of life.

Everyone deserves to live a life of greatness and fulfillment. You should live the type of life that gives you passion and purpose for getting up every day and facing the world. God promises that we can have a more abundant life. Don't cheat, steal, and rob yourself of life. "The thief cometh not, but for to steal, and to kill, and to destroy: I am come that they might have life, and that they might have it more abundantly" (John 10:10).

I can tell you that my promised land is being able to have complete control over my life and doing what God has called me to do with this life he has given me. My promised land is helping other women in fulfilling their goals and birthing their dreams. I don't think that I have fully arrived to my promised land, but I feel I am on the street and my destination is only blocks away. I never imaged the life that I am living; I don't mean that in a physical sense, but from a mental perspective. Many people are taught to finish high school and get a job and that if they accomplish those two things, they will be set for life. I believe that could have been my story. I sit and wonder some days, thinking, *How does a young fifteen-year-old teenage mother from the projects get to live bicoastally? How does this teenage mother from the projects get to decide what days she wants to work for others and what state she wants to do it in? How does this teenage mother from the projects get to decide when and where she would like to go on vacation? How does this teenage mother from the projects get to decide what days she wants to stay in bed and click her remote all day?* Well, that part sounds good, but anyone who knows me knows I don't stay still very long. But the bottom line of what I am saying is, how does one have that kind of control over one's life? Planning—making a recipe and a road map for your life. This life that I am living did not happen by accident. It took a lot of hard work, and I had to plan, write, and rewrite my recipe and road map. Yes, I have had many roads of victory, but I have also shed many tears of failure and defeat. But one thing I do understand is that "we know that all things work together for good to them that love God, to them who are the called according to his purpose" (Romans 8:28).

Reaching your promised land will give you feelings of completion, satisfaction, joy, and inner peace. I hope that you have started writing or rewriting your recipe and road map.

You never know what is waiting for you!

CHAPTER 10 REFLECTION

What do you think about your promised land?

Looking at Maslow's hierarchy of needs, how high have you reached?

Do you think you deserve to reach your promised land?

Tonya Latney

"I just want to do God's will. And he's allowed me to go to the mountain. And I've looked over, and I've seen the Promised Land! I may not get there with you, but I want you to know tonight that we as a people will get to the Promised Land".

Martin Luther King, Jr.

PERSONAL REFLECTIONS

Thank you for taking the time to read my book. I hope that it has inspired you to change things in your life or to give it to someone whom you think needs to be inspired.

As I was writing this book, it came to a point where the Devil was walking on my heels, probably because he knew that one or more women might be set free by reading it. You see, when God calls you to the battlefield and places you on the front line that means you have to fight. I was coming to the end of this journey, and I had to take off the heels and dresses and put on the jeans and T-shirts, put my hair in a ponytail, and take my earrings out—and yes, I had to put Vaseline on my face. The enemy sent opposition in different ways to stop what I had been called to do. I knew that I was in a fight, but guess what? This chick from the projects was not about to let the enemy win. During this fight, I was hit so hard it knocked me to my knees. I started to wave the towel to say I'd had enough, but I realized this fight was not about me. That voice inside of me kept saying, "You can't give up!" If you are going to fall, land on your back, because if you can look up, you can get up. Somebody might need to grab your hand, but you can get up. So just remember that getting to your promised land may be a fight, but God will camp angels on your path to see to it that you make it to your promised land. You will win!

Trust me on this one.

If you were one of the angels that God placed on my path, thank you!

I would love your feedback on the book please visit me at http://www.tonyalatney.com/

A portion of the proceeds from the book will be donated to Achievability

http://www.achieveability.org/about-us.html

ENDNOTES

i   H. Stanley Judd

ii   Christopher Morley

iii   Franklin Delano Roosevelt, inaugural speech (Washington, DC, March 4, 1933), http://history.eserver.org/fdr-inaugural.txt.

iv   Chin Ning Chu

v   Charles Lindbergh

vi   Bessie Stanley

vii   "Beautiful," PoemsAbout.com, http://www.poemsabout.com/beautiful/.

viii   "Maslow's Heirarchy of Needs," Learning-Theories.com, http://www.learning-theories.com/maslows-hierarchy-of-needs.html.

http://www.brainyquote.com/quotes/keywords/promised_land.html

www.ingramcontent.com/pod-product-compliance
Lightning Source LLC
Chambersburg PA
CBHW060817050426
42449CB00008B/1706